D0897856

Anne & Alpheus

1842–1882

Anne & Alpheus

1842–1882

Joe Survant (signature)

— JOE SURVANT —

To Bill and Celia
with best wishes.
JS
12/23/96

THE UNIVERSITY OF ARKANSAS PRESS

Fayetteville 1996

Copyright 1996 by Joe Survant

All rights reserved

Manufactured in the United States of America

oo   99   98   97   96   5   4   3   2   1

Designed by Gail Carter

☺ The paper used in this publication meets the
minimum requirements of the American
National Standard for Permanence of Paper for
Printed Library Materials z39.48-1984.

Library of Congress Cataloging-in-Publication Data
Survant, Joe, 1942–
    Anne & Alpheus, 1842–1882 / Joe Survant.
      p.   cm.
   ISBN 1-55728-415-6 (cloth : alk. paper). —
   ISBN 1-55728-416-4 (pbk. : alk. paper)
   1. Married people—Kentucky—Poetry.
   2. Farm Life—Kentucky—Poetry.
   3. Kentucky—History—Poetry.   I. Title.
PS3569.U728A56 1996   95-36192
811'.54—dc20   CIP

For Jeannie

Acknowledgments

"Anne Waters: August 9, 1842," "Alpheus
Waters: August 9, 1842," "Anne Waters:
October 20, 1842," "Alpheus Waters: November
15, 1842," "Anne Waters: December 24, 1842,"
and "Alpheus Waters: December 29, 1842" were
published in *Nimrod* and were an Honorable
Mention for the Pablo Neruda Prize in 1991.
"Anne Waters: September 2, 1862" and
"Alpheus Waters: August 27, 1863" were also
published in *Nimrod* in 1995. "Anne Waters: May
1, 1882" was published in *The American Voice* in
1994, retitled "Anniversary" and slightly revised
to stand independently. The first section of *Anne
& Alpheus: 1842–1882* was published as a chap-
book, with the title *We Will All Be Changed,* by
State Street Press in 1995. *Anne & Alpheus:
1842–1882* was a finalist in the 1994 *Texas Review*
Press competition, in the 1994 Anhinga Poetry
Prize competition, and for the 1992 Ohio State
University Press/ *The Journal* Award. A selection
of poems from *Anne & Alpheus: 1842–1882* was
the runner-up for the Robert H. Winner Award
from the Poetry Society of America in 1994, a
finalist for the Baxter Hathaway Prize from
Epoch in 1993, and a finalist for the *New Letters*
Poetry Prize in 1991.

Contents

I. 1842–1843

Anne Waters AUGUST 9, 1842 3

Alpheus Waters AUGUST 9, 1842 4

Alpheus Waters AUGUST 15, 1842 6

Anne Waters SEPTEMBER 1, 1842 8

Alpheus Waters SEPTEMBER 20, 1842 10

Anne Waters SEPTEMBER 21, 1842 11

Alpheus Waters SEPTEMBER 22, 1842 12

Anne Waters SEPTEMBER 22, 1842 14

Anne Waters OCTOBER 9, 1842 16

Alpheus Waters OCTOBER 12, 1842 17

Anne Waters OCTOBER 20, 1842 19

Alpheus Waters OCTOBER 22, 1842 21

Anne Waters OCTOBER 31, 1842 23

Anne Waters NOVEMBER 3, 1842 25

Alpheus Waters NOVEMBER 12, 1842 27

Anne Waters NOVEMBER 15, 1842 29

Alpheus Waters NOVEMBER 15, 1842 31

Anne Waters DECEMBER 1, 1842 33

Alpheus Waters DECEMBER 20, 1842 35

Anne Waters DECEMBER 24, 1842 37

Anne Waters DECEMBER 28, 1842 39

Alpheus Waters DECEMBER 29, 1842 41

Anne Waters DECEMBER 31, 1842 43

Alpheus Waters JANUARY 1, 1843 45

II. 1862–1863

Alpheus Waters	AUGUST 15, 1862	*49*
Alpheus Waters	AUGUST 16, 1862	*51*
Anne Waters	AUGUST 20, 1862	*53*
Alpheus Waters	AUGUST 23, 1862	*55*
Anne Waters	SEPTEMBER 2, 1862	*56*
Alpheus Waters	SEPTEMBER 10, 1862	*58*
Isaac	SEPTEMBER 26, 1862	*59*
Alpheus Waters	SEPTEMBER 26, 1862	*61*
Alpheus Waters	OCTOBER 9, 1862	*63*
Anne Waters	OCTOBER 15, 1862	*65*
Alpheus Waters	NOVEMBER 3, 1862	*67*
Isaac	NOVEMBER 15, 1862	*69*
Sarah	NOVEMBER 20, 1862	*70*
Anne Waters	DECEMBER 21, 1862	*72*
Anne Waters	JANUARY 26, 1863	*74*
Alpheus Waters	FEBRUARY 20, 1863	*75*
Anne Waters	FEBRUARY 20, 1863	*77*
Anne Waters	MAY 1, 1863	*79*
Anne Waters	JUNE 21, 1863	*82*
Anne Waters	AUGUST 27, 1863	*83*
Alpheus Waters	AUGUST 27, 1863	*85*
Alpheus Waters	SEPTEMBER 2, 1863	*87*
Anne Waters	SEPTEMBER 2, 1863	*89*

III. 1881–1882

Anne Waters	DECEMBER 21, 1881	93
Alpheus Waters	DECEMBER 21, 1881	95
Alpheus Waters	FEBRUARY 17, 1882	97
Alpheus Waters	MARCH 10, 1882	99
Alpheus Waters	APRIL 3, 1882	100
Anne Waters	APRIL 4, 1882	101
Anne Waters	APRIL 27, 1882	102
Anne Waters	MAY 1, 1882	103
Anne Waters	MAY 15, 1882	104
Alpheus Waters	MAY 16, 1882	106
Alpheus Waters	JUNE 5, 1882	107
Alpheus Waters	JUNE 19, 1882	109
Alpheus Waters	JULY 12, 1882	111
Alpheus Waters	JULY 13, 1882	113
Anne Waters	JULY 16, 1882	115
Anne Waters	SEPTEMBER 1, 1882	116
Anne Waters	SEPTEMBER 7, 1882	117

I. 1842–1843

For death is come up into our windows,
and is entered into our palaces,
to cut off the children from without,
and the young men from the streets.

JEREMIAH 9:21

Anne Waters

My God, I almost
lost her yesterday.
The infernal heat settled
like a poison in her bones.
I took her to the shade
of our great oak.
There I saw a hawk
rising from the weeds
with this summer's rabbit
crying in his claws.
But I held on tight
and the shadow of the tree
became larger than the tree
and blotted out the sky
and the hawk and the sound
of the rabbit's cry.
She stopped fretting.
When Alph came
we put on the drawing mustard
and the cooling camphor,
but I kept her here
in the shadow of the oak
and watched the sky
all day long.

Alpheus Waters

AUGUST 9, 1842

For weeks now
the sun has been
like the angry eye of God.
Cattle droop in the field
and we sleep in the yard.
Death has crept up
to the horse lot
and waits his chance.
Catherine's first birthday
came and went in the
heat, a year
of colic, whooping cough
and tooth fever biles.
Yesterday, cramps
and nausea took her.
When I came she was
stiller than the
windless air, a cold
but breathing corpse.
We feared cholera,
yet she survives.

Lucas Dillon died last week.
I found him vomiting and purging
in great pain.
Blind and deaf
he was colder than death
but cried out with heat
and suffocation.

We tried poultices and rubs
but the fever would not break.
In the final pain
he shouted glory,
that he could see home
and was ready to go.
I know I should be strengthened
but I fear death
for me and mine.

Alpheus Waters

Another day of
hard sun,
and tobacco wilts
in the fields.
Isaac and I droop too,
stooping after worms
and suckers, a good
crop of them
while our yield's
been cut by half.

The dry ground
the close sticky plants
the heat, like a
hard religion through
whose cathedral we
crawl tending its
stunted fruit.
I fear I've lost
my fire and zeal
to this heat, and
my own religion
grows cold and dry.

Two days ago
I preached over
Aunt Susan before
we laid her in
her long home

in the ground.
For now shall I
sleep in the dust
and thou shalt seek me
in the morning,
but I shall not be.

Cold and heat.
My skin burns
from the touch of tobacco.
Sun heats the air
between the rows
like an oven,
but my mind steps aside
and watches us
like a distant god.

Anne Waters

SEPTEMBER 1, 1842

Two years ago today
we were married.
This should be a happy day
but the heat has still
not broken
and yesterday
Maude Sanders died.
I helped prepare
her for the grave.
I cannot shake the film
that seems a part of heat
and does not lift
when we lie down to sleep.
Two years ago
Alph and I,
and now Catherine,
bine, bole, and bower.
We've grown around
each other like honeysuckle
among morning glories.
The shadows of drifting
clouds touch us briefly
to relieve the morning sun,
and meadowlarks
still sing in the fields.
The years stretch out
before us
like a westward prairie
waving with grass.

The three of us
move through it,
a little schooner
searching for treasure
and some unheard of spice.

Alpheus Waters
SEPTEMBER 20, 1842

Tomorrow I go
to Bethlehem Church.
Still no rain
and the land
shrivels like a
milkweed pod.
I have sat alone
and prayed for
some bit of strength
to help that congregation.
But I cannot
help myself.
I think God has
disappeared into the
sun, his eye,
and stares down blankly
on us.
And there is nothing hid
from the heat thereof.
I will make
a sermon to hide my fears.
Thou hast been a shadow
from the heat.
But my heart
has dried up.
And I search in vain
for words
that will fall
like cooling rain.

Anne Waters

SEPTEMBER 21, 1842

All night I heard
him in the house
and felt him
in the yard.
He left this morning,
tiredness on him
like a cloak.
I wish I could
tell him that I
see fall moving
toward us. In graceful
measure shake back
her hair and bathe
us all in cool autumnal
light.
If we could just
open this heat like
a nut, so the secret
kernel could grow
into mists and mellowness.
I almost feel it
grows in me,
a stone gathering light
in some shallow, rocky pool.
Yet though we are one
Alph works his work
and I mine.
The cow moans
in the shed.
The baby cries.

Alpheus Waters

SEPTEMBER 22, 1842

Instead of rain
I found a rock
and beat and beat
Bethlehem into Golgotha.
I think I am half crazed
and beat all the harder
because of it,
as if they hadn't enough
of wrath on their own.
He shall flee from the iron
weapon and the bow of steel
shall strike him through.
The heat, the drought,
the deaths of children
have left them stunned.
They were not sad
to see me go.

Dust rises around my buggy
until I choke.
Tupper plods on in blindness.
John McCulloch's corn
rustles like blasphemous tongues.
I must shed this despair
settled thick upon me.
Anne, Catherine . . .

The oak, our house
stand waiting
while I move toward them,
a small, isolate storm
floating on shifting
columns of dust
and driven by its
own secret engine.

Anne Waters

I filled the tub
from the well
now down to forty feet.
At first he seemed
all right; Catherine's patter
Papa perty, Papa perty
lifted him as he came in.
He sat in the tub
as docile as my baby
while I poured bucket
after bucket over his head.
Something dark came off
with the dust
and lay in the bottom
of the tub.
We dumped the water
in the garden,
though nothing much
was left but
stunted corn and
a few small tomatoes
gleaming in the grass.
In the late light
I could see
that it had not
all come off.
A grayness on his skin
that I could not
scrub away.

Deeper than fever,
a kind of absence
had entered
when I looked away.
It is so hard always
to be on guard.
First Catherine,
now Alph.
And I can't get
it out.
I will hold him
in bed tonight
and rock and rock
drawing on him
like a poultice
on a fever.

Anne Waters

Tupper and Maria
run before us
opening and closing
like great fists.
The carriage and
road sing together
and the air is cool.
Rain at last
in the night.
No flood but the
cooling wind,
and this morning
we have our mists
and mellowness.
Fall is a woman,
the warm days
her comfort,
the chilly nights
her strength.
And all
over all
lies her light.

Alpheus Waters

I should have known!
My pride in two
strong horses,
the coolness in the air,
the steep hill before
John Finley's house,
the breast straps
wearing on the tongue
too long unchecked
until the carriage
pressed down upon
the horses, and Maria's
eyes rolled whitely
and she broke out
the tongue. Anne
kept herself and Catherine
tight in the seat,
and I held on.
Only Tupper saved us.
I think he would be
steady if all of us
had come down upon him.

Now I watch him
and Maria grazing
calmly by the creek.
I whistle and they
raise their heads and ears.
Sometimes I think I

could go and live
with horses,
take up their dumb strength
and quiet ways.
Then take
my wife and child
on my back
and go fast and far
beyond this year
which gathers around us
with days
of unknown intention.

Anne Waters

OCTOBER 20, 1842

Hogs in the corn!
Sarah and I up
and out with sticks.
They scatter and
make us drive them
one by one,
the squeal of struck
pig flesh,
the rustle of dry corn.
I wonder do they sense
the coming killing time,
out on a last splurge
before the morning
of the knife,
sometime after first
frost.
Though I curse them
now, I shrink
from their messy
pig deaths,
squeals, bawls and
butchering.
Alph says that I
would starve us
if left to follow
feeling.
If only they could
lie down
and give up their flesh

bloodlessly.
And we could take
the meat
as a gift from
some wild tribe
whom we once knew
but no longer understand.

Alpheus Waters

Yesterday I found
poor Tom Cade
dying in great fear.
We prayed and I
tried to comfort him.
What time I am afraid,
I will trust in thee . . .
I will not fear what
flesh can do unto me.
When the shudder
took him, I
held his hand
and watched him
sink into
a great, black pool
and disappear from sight.
I helped prepare him
for the grave
and rode on home
in night.

Then I dreamed
he had not died,
that he and I
swam together
in a dark lake,
that we laughed about
the afternoon's mistake.
But Tom swam on ahead

still laughing
at my fright.
Evening settled around me.
Redwing blackbirds
began to call.
The lake hummed
with hidden life.
Tom swam on strongly,
far beyond my sight.

Anne Waters

Pigeons
by the thousands
in our poor corn.
Rising and falling
in the field
with a great
rustling of wings.
The men have
slaughtered them
by the bushelfuls.
Mann Norton's cannon
loaded with nails
swept birds
from the sky like
a broom, pigeons
wheeling around
the sudden holes it made.
All afternoon the ground
was covered with the dead
and dying, the
hogs gorging on the
still-warm flesh,
the Negro women picking
among them for stew pots
and pies.
After the shooting
hawks came
for the wounded,
big redtails and

humpbacked chicken hawks
brooding over the field.
I thought I'd had
my fill of killing
but remembered the hawk
rising from the dry field
and called to Alph
to bring his gun,
while in my ears
the noise of
one hundred thousand wings
was like a terrible whispering.

Anne Waters

Nights of frost
and the moon filling,
soon the week
of killing hogs
will come.
Already they fatten
in what's left
of the corn lying
in the field
Sarah and I
once chased them from.
Now we watch them
gorging on the yellow
corn, and even
throw out a few ears
from the crib.
Catherine squeals
with pleasure as they
run to Sarah's
Pig, Pig, Pig-ee!
Catherine too has
fattened after a hard
first year. Her new
strength and the
bright days drive her
through the house and yard
and she dogs Sarah
about her chores.
This is my time too,

the splendid passage
between heat and cold
when summer has not
quite let go
and the fields mellow
and all the trees glow
in their silent
sap-deaths.
The light sharpens,
the pigs move through
the corn.
The afternoons
grow intense,
their clear air
lights up the ground
like thought,
yet casts such a
deep and perfect shade.

Alpheus Waters
NOVEMBER 12, 1842

Last night
the wind stripped
the trees
and made a
storm of leaves
driven in
under the door,
and the stable is full.
Trees gestured to us
all night like
lunatics in the yard.
We made taffy
and pretended cheer,
but Anne has paid
dearly for the sweets.
Her teeth began to ache.
The wind blew and blew
her pain and she
cried like her baby.
Tansy and vinegar
gave some relief
toward dawn
and she slept.

With the sun,
the pain again.
Now even laudanum
is in vain.
She has entered

a private room
where no one can
follow. Pain has
blossomed around
her like a rare
flower whose incense
fills the air
and closes off the breath.
Outside the leaves
are still,
and all the trees
are bare.

Anne Waters

Squeals, blood
the sickening hammer
thud. I must be
clear about it,
else I cannot do it.
Sarah, Ellen, and I,
the scalding water
and dull knives.
Alph and Isaac
and Clet, the hammer
and keener knives.
We ready the water
scalding but not
on the boil. The great
black kettle's breath
mingles with the morning
mists. Behind us
the pig squeals
then falls.
Without looking
I see Isaac's
hands at the throat
suddenly washed in blood.
The men dip the body
heavier than a man.
We scrape
with our knives.
Dip, scrape
dip, scrape.

My arms begin to ache,
and then it's done.
Quicker than I
can believe
Isaac frees
the hamstrings
for the gambling stick
and then the hog
is hung.
He kneels,
then moves his hand
gently, carefully
and the hog's secret
blossoms like a flower
from the parting flesh
and falls into a tub
where we too must
kneel to seek liver
heart and lungs
among the blood
and leafing fat.

Alpheus Waters

NOVEMBER 15, 1842

Cold and the moon
full, soon the
smell of meat curing
on the shelves.
But now,
now we have
a week of killing to do.
I'll be glad
when it is done.

Clet and I hold
the first of twenty
while steady Isaac
brings the hammer down.
The women scrape
and ready lard
and sausage pots.
We work well
though Anne's not
pleased with this labor
of blood.

Isaac working with his knife,
seeking the jugular
left side, three inches
down. Turning to the
whetstone before exposing
hamstrings for the stick.
Then, kneeling, with the

carefulest of motions
cuts the stomach
not the sack
until the guts
fall free into the tub.
The head cut
and twisted free
from its heavy body,
the headless body
hanging from the pole.

Clet butchers.
The women tend
their fires and begin
to cook.
The pigs knock
against each other
in their pen.
Isaac motions
and we begin again.

Anne Waters

That week has passed.
I think the cold, clear
air has washed us clean
at last,
and the year wears
down gracefully.
The black arms of
bare trees seem friendly.
The smokehouse shelves
are full and smoke
lies like gray breath
around the door.
Catherine thrives.
Alph's black mood
has lightened, and
I slide in quiet joy
toward Christmas.
Each day is new.
Our pond has become
a mirror,
so still that in
it I see bass
and jays swimming
in a common air.
I could open a door
and enter this world
where birds fly through
heavy air
and fish sit

upon a branch
and sing.
But I have dreamed
the world right through
and sit here
by the water's edge
where blue meets blue,
and the mockingbird rings.

Alpheus Waters

DECEMBER 20, 1842

Gray, and the
first dust of snow
to make it seem
like Christmas.
I take my gun
down to the corn
where daily
migrating ducks
trespass my field.
I have made myself
a blind of stalks
and wait for their return.

A small gang circles.
I do not move.
When their wings set
and they glide in
I rise and shoot.
Two crumple
then bounce on the
hard ground.

A welcome change
from pork
on Christmas day,
but Catherine mourns
their bright feathers
bloodied by the shot.
Sarah takes them out

to clean
while Catherine sits crying
in my lap,
her eyes too bright
her tears too free.
A rising fever blossoms
on her skin.

Anne Waters

Too much killing.
We live by death
and now the messy
deaths of animals
have entered the
house, and I cannot
hide her. Four nights
of fever and now
a fifth. A dry cough
wastes her little strength
and nothing helps.
Helpless, we watch her
blur and fade.
I would give back
all the blood and
flesh and become
like cattle grazing
in the passive grain
if I could pick
her up and shake
the awful brightness
from her eyes,
her mind flaring
while the body dies.
I look out at
my great oak tree,
but its heart is empty

and its arms full
of brittle air.
In the woods I
see the falling snow
and hear the hunting owl.

Anne Waters

DECEMBER 28, 1842

She is gone.
A door in the earth
opened. She
fell through
our lives and
entered it. I
would have followed
but Alph and Mama
stopped me. The
door closed heavy
above her and I
could not go.
Now nature stands
between us, the
dark cedars an
admonition, and a
wall. For three days
I've sought that door,
felt along the smooth
earth for
fast-fading edges,
Alph and God
standing in my way.
Then I find it.
I cross the meadow
in the worn track
of cattle where
it lies gleaming
dully in the winter

light. The cold makes
my feet ache, but I give
myself to it, sinking slowly
into silence and
what I hope is light.

Alpheus Waters
DECEMBER 29, 1842

Will this wretched
year ever end?
First Catherine,
now Anne pulled
struggling against us
from the pond.
If Sarah had not
seen her . . .
Now she lies wrapped
in blankets by the
fire, still held
in some dream of
finding our lost child.

I have grieved until
I'm dry and tears
come hard now.
Surely the bitterness of death
is past. I seek
solace from God
and read the words.
For the trumpet shall sound
and the dead shall be raised
incorruptible, and we shall
be changed. But change
is all I see, and in
this world I've had enough
of change.

I go out to feed the
horses. They rush up
to me, grateful
and full of their
dumb lives. The warm
smell of hay is
a blessing in the cold.

Anne Waters

Such a stormy night!
The wind comes in
at every crack, and makes
the chimney howl
and drives
the smoke within.
The leafless limbs
of forest oak lie
about the yard.
The year is dying
a hard death.
We cannot sleep
and sit to see
the new year in.
There is some breach
between us,
a piece of stoney meadow
that I have crossed
and have not crossed
again.
In my mind
I lean toward him
with all my might
even though we already
sit before the fire
under a common blanket.
We embrace,
but the wind
makes a hideous sound

like some dumb
creature being
slaughtered in the night
and I cannot rest
or keep her
from my sight.

Alpheus Waters

JANUARY 1, 1843

Blue, so blue
and cold and clean
that last night
is wiped away
except for the litter
of limbs in the yard
and the shingles
gone from the shed.
We walk through
the cold,
Anne still with the look
of someone stunned
but her eyes are clear.

The wind blew
like a wind from
hell last night
but left this dome
of crystal air, and
the Indian grass
sparkles with rime
that's fading fast.
The horses emerge
from the shed,
their frozen breaths
hanging about them
like little low clouds.

Now is the time to
try the words again.
Behold, I shew you a mystery;
we shall not all sleep,
but we shall all be changed.
We turn then
to watch our smoke
rising toward the
high ceiling of
wide, incorruptible sky.

II. 1862–1863

And when ye shall hear of wars and rumours of wars, be ye not troubled: for such things must needs be; but the end shall not be yet.

MARK 13:7

Alpheus Waters

All we have is
a confounding shimmer
of this and that.
Morgan's at Glasgow
and Red River bridge burned.
All the while
soldiers pass
backward and forward
on the rails.
The war and rumors
of war swirl around us
like the Barren in flood.
God has turned away
and we live daily
in the merely human.

Anne and I
huddle here
on Whippoorwill Creek.
Cattle make their
same slow rounds.
Crops rise and
fall in the bottoms
and we come and go.
In the meadow
wild mustard shines
and the creek
murmurs its promise.
But each night

a comet hangs
in the northwestern sky
like a streak of blood,
and in the day
soldiers wither and die
in the fields.

Alpheus Waters

When I first saw him
I could not believe
who it was.
The Tom Shaw who
rode off to join
the Rebels is gone,
youth sucked from
him like marrow
from a bone,
his right leg
removed by a minnie
ball at Bull Run.
We shall not soon
be rid of this war.
It has settled in
to stay like bad
weather, and will
not lift.

I wonder where
God is in all of this?
Both sides claim him.
Yet both are swept
away. Rebels and
Federals spring up
like Tom Shaws
in the morning,
and in the evening
are cut down.

Shall he that planted
the ear, not hear?
He that formed the eye,
shall he not see?

All I can see
is grayish Tom Shaw
moving like an old
man along the road,
his father's land
wasting beneath the sun,
the rain falling on us all.

Anne Waters

I have turned around
and now
am forty.
The days have quickened
and run before me
down a narrow forest path.
A covey of quail
explodes from a
thicket as I pass by,
and corn flowers
flair and fade
along the way.
Where I once saw prairie
and a steady sailing
there is the stop and start
of thicket and briar,
lit occasionally by
the green light of
meadows and glens.
For twenty-one years
Alph and I have grown together,
an oak and maple
mingling canopies
above the tangled floor,
roots twining
in the same ground.
But each close within
its hull of bark
made hard by

weather and ways.
I rise each morning
and walk out.
The dawn is fair yet,
and the sky sends
clouds sailing out
like promises that
can still be kept.

Alpheus Waters

AUGUST 23, 1862

I stand alone at the edge
of a ten acre field
with tomahawk and spear,
knowing it must all be cut
one stalk at a time
and speared on a tobacco stick.
Bend, push, twist, lift.
The eye and hand just right.

Slowly I move down a row
through spiders, flies, and worms.
The war has taken the help I need
to harvest other fields
and irrigate them, too.
Youth flows into the war
like water down a hole.

All day the plants
raise their arms
before me in the heat.
Behind me their bodies
lie upon the field.

Anne Waters
SEPTEMBER 2, 1862

I fingered it so long,
like a child a scab,
that it almost didn't heal.
But after twenty years
even the worst
wound turns
dry and smooth.
Twenty childless years
and now nature
closes the door.
Alph and I have
ridden the stream
through mid-flood.
Now the water
begins to fall,
the creek settles
into its stoney cage.
Slaughter is such
a habit now,
I doubt it'll
pass us by.
David Small killed
at Bull Run,
Maude living off
the charity of neighbors.
We must help each
other or die
I fear, but the
war comes between us.

And now word
of another Bull Run
as if the ground
had grown thirsty
again, and needed
its drink of blood.
The path to the place
we laid her
is worn like the
track of cattle.
The little redbud
I planted there
has spread and
grown a tree
and wild grasses
have long since
sown up the earth.
How long to heal
the wounds of war?
The battle-raised
blood of it
has touched us all
and will appear
and reappear
like a defect
working through
the generations.

Alpheus Waters

SEPTEMBER 10, 1862

Twenty feet above
the hard dirt floor
the flimsy tier poles
tremble. The sharp
smell of burley in the
dusty heat is overwhelming,
but balanced here
in the housing of tobacco,
between the poles
and hanging plants, I feel
the power of labor's
pure intention. High up
near the roof beams
where crisp-bodied
mud daubers follow their
closely reasoned paths
and worlds of dust
are shook loose in shafts
of light, I could almost
step into this space
of heavy air and
quietly curing plants.
But once, at fourteen,
a pole gave way, and
delivered of my breath
I came back to the
thick earth and its strict
catechism of the senses,
blood, bone, and sinew.

Isaac

I'd never even
heard a white man
say the word before.
But there it was
hanging in the air
like The Word
in The Beginning.
Maybe they're the same.
It took freedom
to say *Let*
there be light
and cancel out
that endless night.

We were with the
horses, back from
Owensville. The town
stirring and roiling
with rumor.
He watched me
take the harness
off Dan.
What would you do
with freedom, Isaac?
How'd you and Sarah live?
I could not speak
or even see. The word
used up all my senses.
I could even smell

its honeysuckle sound.
Dan stamped and snorted
at his half unleashing.
Becky's patience was
about to end.
I turned to him and said
Why, Mr. Waters,
we'd be free.

Alpheus Waters

It was a mistake
to take him with me
into town. The place
hummed with
Have you heard,
have you heard what
Lincoln might do?
It's not good for
him to hear
such talk. It fuels
hope with rumor
and aggravates dissatisfaction.

I could tell it
worked on him. His body
sat beside me and
held the reins.
Even the horses
sensed an absent hand
and pulled against each
other half the time.
His mind was already
with the others who rarely
get to town. Yet
how can they understand
what they've never known?
How can they live
away from here?

When I heard his answer
in the barn,
this Sunday's text
filled me and I
could not speak.
He hath sent me
to heal the brokenhearted,
to preach deliverance to the
captives.

I think we both
had trouble talking
in this new knowledge
of our bond.
Slave, master, freedom.
How can I say them and
speak those words of Christ?
So I used others
and imagined them content.
Now I see we'll need
a new vocabulary
and with the words
will come a rearranging
of intent.
No, we'll need
a whole new language.
First the word
and then the act.

Alpheus Waters

The war is like
a great drama
and we watch first
this act and then another.
Rumors fall like curtains—
Washington is lost,
Louisville surrounded,
Nashville burned—
then lift suddenly
to reveal some fact
that glistens
with ambiguity.
Kentucky is filled
with dark sentiments
and divided selves.

Last Monday
Federals seized
Cash Johnson's William,
put him on a horse
stolen from Dr. Hill,
strapped a gun on him
and forced him away
despite his protests.
Many others freely go.
Federals retreating
from Nashville have
left hundreds of Negroes
begging from people
who cannot feed themselves.

Isaac and Sarah
grow restless.
We have words.
I think that they
will leave soon,
to find God knows what.
The bonds of faith
and work
still join us
but are weakened
by the day,
and all the while
the fact of ownership
festers between us
like an unhealed sore.

Anne Waters

I think our time
is a crucible
where change is
daily brewed.
I could not believe
it of her. Mary
my girlhood friend
barring Federals from
her door with a
Bowie knife, saying
she was willing to
die if her
murder would fill
up Rebel ranks.
I do not know
if I can still drink
from the same well
as her, yet our
girlhood was filled
with oaths of love
and we both once
stood alone and lost
but unafraid
in Tom Miller's
darkening woods.
But now I'm
stuck between hard
unyielding loss and
a quickening rate of change.

What is it that
barters away the
child for winding
mossy ways, and
days that pile
on days?

Alpheus Waters

NOVEMBER 3, 1862

Mischief shall come upon mischief,
and rumour shall be upon rumour . . .
but the law shall perish . . .

Isaac came home
from town
with a strange tale.
Ten horsemen claiming
to be Morgan's men
fleeing Federal cavalry
passed through Whitesville
this morning. They said
they'd killed the guard at
Elkhorn bridge, fired it,
and now sought the way
to Jamestown. They
were caught before
afternoon, not raiders,
merely horse thieves
hiding behind the war.

So it goes.
Our life's diurnal
course rocketed by
volleys of rumor
which light up
our nights and
disturb our days
with a strange
and fitful glare.

At 3 A.M.
Sam Hines sent
for me to help
console his wife,
ill and afraid of dying.
I found her in a
nervous fit and crying
I'm almost gone.
Lost. So wicked.
When I tried to pray
with her she cried
Too late! Too late!
I believe the hysteria
of the country
has touched us all,
though ill
she's neither wicked
nor dying.

Isaac

There's been some
change in the way
we speak,
he less likely to order
me less likely to obey.
I think we've come up
on each other some,
so that the dry creek
rises until it fits
its banks once more.
And now we adjust ourselves
and await more rain.
Soon the flood will come,
lifting first the
dry driftwood
then cutting out
the banks below
the water-loving maples
and sweeping all away.
Sarah and I must
make ourselves a raft
so that we can ride
the crest
into some place
where we define the
space, and measure
out our time.

Sarah

NOVEMBER 20, 1862

I like the way
they come and go,
those saucy jays,
and one day Isaac
and I too will
sprout wings and
fly away with
Dolly and Robert
to Louisville
where Negroes wear
fine clothes and live
in brick homes
and stroll along
the streets in
the late afternoons.
I will be sad
to leave her,
though there's sorrow
and something of envy
when she watches
me soothing Dolly
over some hurt,
or fixing Robert's food
to carry with him
to the fields.
We've grown up together,
had children,
now begin to age,
but still . . .

I am not like
those jays that
use the yard,
then wheel off
crying in the air.
I mean I cannot.
Once
I thought she might
be like my lost sister,
but that died with
her baby, and Dolly's
growing fine and strong.
Now there's mostly
the thousand times
we baked the bread,
or chased the hogs
from out the corn,
each act a stitch
between us.
And yet,
I still
am owned.

Anne Waters

Dreamed I had my baby
back,
held her in a blanket
before the fire
and rubbed her
arms and legs
until she moved again,
and then began to cry.
I was suddenly
filled up,
like something solid
had entered my body,
or an arm lost long ago
had returned
to swell the empty sleeve and
drive away the phantom pain.
We rocked and rocked
before that fire
which blazed impossibly,
devouring the cold
and pushing back the dark
around the house.
I ran to tell the news,
but when I lifted
the cover there was
only the piglet I'd
tried to save last spring,
already cold and still.
Then I was myself again.

What was here
was still around me,
what was gone
was absent as before.
Outside a cold rain
fell blankly on the roof
and in the empty fields.

Anne Waters

I forgot to move them
in the hurry
of the harvest time.
Now warmed to life
by the January sun
they struggle beneath
bushes whose lives
have overgrown their own.
The sharp insistent crocus spikes
piercing the warming ground
rising from the dull bulbs
I planted here some
twenty years ago,
speaking each spring
in words of purple,
white, and gold.
I do not think they'll
speak to me
for having abandoned
them to their dark sleep
and hard awakening.
I clear their way
as best I can,
pull away the smothering leaves
and trim the overreaching limbs.
Despite neglect
I yet might save
them for another year,
but, oh—
their suffocation
in the ground!

Alpheus Waters

Gone!
While we were
in Owensville,
Isaac and Sarah
Dolly and Robert,
and with them
the wagon and half
the smokehouse stores.
Well, let them have it.
We shared the bloody
work between us.

I should not blame
their going,
yet I do,
the deception of it.
Somewhere words failed,
more likely were not spoken.
The unsaid
like fine cracks
spreading through ice
under great strain.

I do not know
how such solitude
will sit,
Anne silent
in her kitchen
while I work

alone in the barn.
Yet they must go
their way,
black from white,
resolving the gray.

Such stillness now.
Anne fixes supper
while I milk the cow.
The warm beast-smell
fills the stable's air.
In the dusk
I lean my head
against Bessie's side.
She stands compliant
while I work,
quiet in the
stolid way of cows.

Anne Waters

I knew they'd go
from the way Sarah
kneaded dough
and washed the pans,
absently,
already distracted
by Louisville's heady glow.
I wanted to speak,
to tell her no
not that way
among strangers
in a place they did
not know,
away from a life
lived close at hand
among things that
can be known
and work that can
be done.
Alph says it's land,
rather the lack of it.
There's no tie
just pointless chores
for some other man.
Surely Sarah felt
the rhythm that I feel,
the gathering of the corn
the baking of the bread
winter falling into spring

evening into early morning.
But war and change
have settled all
around us,
so that the old life
which we have worn
already seems a dream,
and a new way
already born.

Anne Waters

MAY 1, 1863

It's like a flaw
in a glass pane.
When I move,
the world is bent.
Is it things
have changed,
the world grown
new limbs,
or me?
Yet the time too
is like a lens I
have not used before,
calling up another
world beside me.
Somewhere
between the two
I make my way
through chores and days,
learning to live with
strangeness.
Ida Pell
mildest of my friends
now threatens neighbors
who will not take
the oath
and sees a Rebel
in us all.
Ida with her fine
rum cake,

her hands once ready
to share,
keeps herself close
and hardens against us.
The swarming bees we labored
to save in the orchard
divided again
and flew away.
We found them a mile off,
high up a hickory,
and brought them back
and hope that they
will stay.
The dark honey
from the hive
glistens dull as
amber in the pan,
its overripe taste
lingers like a memory
of earth and darkness.
Beneath its surface
a strange face
peers up at me.
It is a night
of dreaming, where
we wake to dream
more, and hardly
know the difference.
Somehow we must

hold on to the circuit
of things so that
rock and field
and tree and house
are markers
for our wandering
and borders of all
our inner property.

Anne Waters

Because its flesh
is not my flesh
its life not my life,
I am drawn under
its great arms
and the leaves
heavy with green.
Like a small animal
I creep warily to the trunk,
watching earth and air.
Its skin is hard and rough
against my own.
Its life stands still and large.
I dart about
and am never still.
It has stood here so long
I can almost see its heart
which beats so slowly
that Alph and Catherine and I
still work and walk about,
and love our lives.

Anne Waters

Sometimes I feel
water moving
below me.
Streams rushing
through darkness.
Blind pools staring
at sandstone walls.
Some unfathomable mind
at work,
meditating on stones
and night.
Often in hot weather
we go down
where Lost River
falls into the ground,
the cool air
of its disappearance
a blessing in the heat.
But I have felt a chill
that I carry all
the way through the
hot fields of corn,
and lie at night
dreaming of struggling
in that current.
Once I heard
her voice
mingled with the water's,
and ceased struggling

and let the water
take me.
Days after,
I haunted
the stream's side
and listened at the
cavern's mouth.
The water-drawn sycamores
leaned down, too.
But no voice ever
spoke to us.
The water murmured
its usual protest as it
fell, the sandstone
boulders stood their ground,
and the air embraced
the cold.
I cannot speak
to Alph of this.
I hide it
and make it a part of
solitude that grows
inside, like water
disappearing in a hole.

Alpheus Waters

AUGUST 27, 1863

I see it when
we walk back
from the spring,
a tilt away
from me, toward
something she looks at
that I can't see.
No,
more like listens to
in the full sound of
water flowing over
rock, but subtle
like the dust that settles
on corn
when rains don't come.

The anniversary of our
marriage comes round
again, now part of
the motion of a great
wheel that rises
and falls
lifting and dropping
our work and days.

I miss the fierce
yearning of that early time,
the days in anticipation
of the nights,

the pleasure taken
out and savored
for itself,
the hard, irresistible
embrace.

Yet I'd be afraid
to add that fierceness
to the times.
Better to settle
here on the land
with the steadiness
of limestone boulders
slowly weathering
from the ground.

Alpheus Waters
SEPTEMBER 2, 1863

First the black oak
taller than the rest,
then back a quarter mile
to where a patch of ferns
grows round a sinkhole,
and beyond that
the swampy place
where I shot the
big fox squirrel.
Next were hickories,
or was it cedar
then hickory?

Anne was right.
I should have hunted
our familiar woods,
not these endless, monotonous flats
where every tree's the same
and the land offers up no mark.
Still, ten squirrels is
a good day's work,
if I can follow myself out.
The big, shaggy hickory
alive with squirrels
and the ground a carpet of cuttings
must be just past this thicket.
And there's the gum
where I sat and watched awhile,
or was it oak?

The sun has long since
passed from sight
and Anne must be
worrying at the coming night.
The shade of all these leaves
grows thicker.
I can no longer see
the spider webs which
hang from all the boughs.
My eyes burn from them,
and they cling to all my clothes.
My rifle has become a burden.
The lush, soggy air
is filled with the humming
of mosquitoes
and trees seem endless
in the rising night.

Anne Waters

It is as though
I have awakened
in the middle of a long journey
to find myself lost
in a dark woods.
Mama and Catherine
both gone half my life,
yet living in that
life we carry
with us through all
our nights and days.
Am I awake
or do I sleep?
The noise of war
is far away.
I walk along the path
where shade drowns
too softly into shade.
The heavy limbs of oaks
oppress me,
dense thickets of locust
and briar are filled
with anxiety,
while lush maples
droop with regret.
Even the gentle cattle
press against me
and drive me into
the sunless trees.

I have looked long
for a starlit clearing,
for some place where
the canopy is lifted
only for a minute
from this wild
and wooden world.

III. 1881–1882

All the rivers run into the sea;
yet the sea is not full;
unto the place from whence the rivers come,
thither they return again.

ECCLESIASTES 1:7

Anne Waters

Colder still,
and the delicate frost
works its geometry
on all the trees.
Even weeds
and spires of grass
wear frost like ashes
while the simpler snow
lies more than two feet deep
in our level yard.
The roof strains
under the snow's body
and the timbers crack
in the cold.
I ready the oven for
bread we do not need
to help keep off the cold.
My breadboard
shines from use
and I gladly touch
the smooth edges where
oak is joined to oak.
His hands made it
and mine have shaped it
in forty years of work,
and here's the scar
she made once
in play . . .
I hate for Alph

to be out in this,
in the frozen woods
and fallen snow.
I know how
snow swallows
up noise, even
of a man moving
through a woods,
how silence sprouts
from the heart
like hoarfrost from
the ruptured cores of weeds,
how quickly darkness falls.

Alpheus Waters

I follow fresh tracks
through the new snow
and strain to read
their meaning.
But across the woods'
blank pages all they
say is stop and go.
The trail traces
subtle thickets
of brush and briar
while the deer huddle
in their hollow beds
dreaming of acorns and weather.
Between storms they
leave precise messages
in two-pronged prints.

I try again to read
their sign, but think
only of Anne alone
in our warm house
and feel my feet
grow dumb as stumps.
Cedars stand taller
than a wall, their odor
sharp and green.
The deer are silent
behind the trees.

I am baffled by
the snow's blind stare.
What is this body
that I wander in,
this place I wander through?

Alpheus Waters

Old Simon, the Negro who lives
on Henry Ballard's place,
told me a wonderful tale
of coming into this country
with Henry's grandfather,
of losing their way in a
swamp near Green River,
of despairing of ever breaking free,
then coming suddenly
into a fair, wide meadow
and dry woods where deer
grazed docile as cattle,
where bears reared up
curious from blackberries
and rabbits moved from
their path, but did not run.

I think of our woods now,
of the absence of deer
and how the Whippoorwill
which once ran clear
now fills with mud from
our fields with every rain,
and of the scarcity of game,
of the great flocks of pigeons
that once filled the sky taking two
days and a night to pass by.

Though we prosper now
I fear we are sweeping
the earth clean of lives
other than our own
and will come blindly
to a day where
the woods are still
and all the meadows
filled with standing
regiments of corn.

Alpheus Waters

MARCH 10, 1882

The time for tobacco is here
again, and I sift the fine
seeds through my hands.
Though my faith may not be
as a grain of mustard seed,
I hope it will multiply
like these small dark seeds,
two teaspoons spawning
four hundred feet of bed.

With greater effort now
I begin again the spring,
the preparation and the
sowing of the bed.
The rich soil beneath the rake
still cool in the early light,
the long day beneath the sun,
then the canvas like a
sheet over the earthen bed.

In winter I sometimes
anticipate these things,
the seeds lying in the dark earth,
the canvas rising and falling
like a lung, the pale
green plants waiting to begin
their new lives in the sun.

Alpheus Waters

APRIL 3, 1882

I was watching early the dew
drawn off our oats and wheat
by the warming sun when I
heard of Dick Hughes' death.
Anne comforted Helen while
I went for the coffin and
helped Josh to lay him out.

We buried him in his garden
where sweet corn had risen
last spring and pole beans
had wound and rewound
themselves all summer.

I read from John at the grave.
Our friend Lazarus sleepeth,
but I go, that I may awake
him out of sleep.
Helen seemed not to hear,
locked in her room of grief.

He walked out to see his stock,
came back vomiting blood,
was gone before eight.
Another friend lost and
I see how my time
too is run to waste.
I say the words again,
both for Helen's sake
and for my own.

Anne Waters

When I saw her
stricken by the bed
grief filled up my
head and I almost
could not speak.
Helen and Dick,
Alph and I,
a long time.
The hole in the garden
stares blankly
and Helen falters.
I touch her arm
but an invisible bell glass
has fallen round her.
I see her lips move,
the bubble of sorrow
swelling out,
no words but a cry.
Yet the day opens
around us
like a promise.
Snow-on-the-mountain
begins its brief
life in the grass
and the words
Alph reads
fall upon us
like a soft rain.

Anne Waters

On my second pass
by the pond,
after the woods
had yielded up
its weak nightshade
in moist thickets
drooping clusters
green, fast turning
to ruby red,
after the marsh violet
had exposed its
dark-throated petals,
after the cool secret
rooms of wooded bottoms,
the mallards and geese
of our sunny pond
are a welcome crowd.
I am ready
for this society,
to lie resting
in the new grass
having had too much
of the deep woods
and its winding
gloomy ways.
Here by the water
bottlebrush emphatically makes
its point and the
sawtooth oak hardly
casts a shade.

Anne Waters

MAY 1, 1882

The way wood grows
smooth with use,
the way hands
harden against wood,
the way we've worn
around each other.
Alph and I grown
alternately smooth and hard
each shaping and
being shaped
in the play
of will on will.
But now we've
grown peaceful
with old age.
The fire rises, then
falls into itself
making a little
cave of dark.
In the quiet thicket
below the house
honeysuckle in yearly
measure constricts
and winds
by small degrees
the living trunk
of a sassafras tree.

Anne Waters

It's a social thing,
one that I've enjoyed
unlike the bloody work
of killing hogs,
this pulling and transplanting
of the plants.
We could hire it done
but will not give it up
like other chores
because of age.
Alph and I move slowly
with one hired man
pulling plants together
through the bed,
bundling them for
the larger field.
Yet by my side
Sarah and Mary
still crawl beneath the
soft spring sun,
Sarah lost
these twenty years
in Louisville,
and Mary dead
at fifty-one.
We laugh at something
silly, out of the
pure pleasure of work
and the strength

to get it done.
I rise to keep
Catherine out of
the unpulled plants,
she runs past my arms
toward the wooded bottoms
whose precise darkness falls
shade into shade
shutting out the sun.

Alpheus Waters

My hands are yet quick
enough to ride the setter
and I still love the
rhythm of horse, earth, and plants.
We work back and forth
across the field, Bell
pulling like a sail,
me riding in the low seat
placing plants in the waves
the plow turns up.
Tom speaks constantly to Bell.
It is so smoothly done
we finish early
and take our time
with Anne's fine meal.

Tom gone,
we sit in the new shade
of our great oak
to watch the evening come
up from the woods, still soft
with the newness of the year.
Anne watches intently where
blackberry bushes begin
to complicate themselves
with the intricate motives
of fruit.
I look out to the fresh field
where the new tobacco
stands waiting for the night.

Alpheus Waters

JUNE 5, 1882

Mountain Boy parts this
muddy river like a plow,
water washed thick with
topsoil from the fields.
I love the power of its
wheel, and blades that
drive us against the stream
to Hawesville.
Owensboro's yellow banks
have long since fallen behind
and the Ohio lies before us
like an undiscovered land.

Sand Island hides the
Indiana shore and seems
to move with us in the mist.
Blue herons stalk the shallows
taking fish and frogs with
sudden snakelike strikes.
Crows call to each other
in their harsh language
and ducks move by
in tight formations.

Over everything the current flows.
Never losing its patience
it growls past the boat's prow
and makes a wake
at all the snags.

Riding through the river
of air, the sun and moon
cast their own currents
on the water, on the shore,
and on us all.

Alpheus Waters

At the other end of the row
Tom bends slightly to the task
of chopping out the weeds
in our tobacco patch.
The early June morning
rises in a mist around us,
its coolness a false promise
in the coming heat.
The hoe's handle hard and
smooth with work slides
easily through my hands,
but I know that Tom
and I will meet in my
half of the row.
He works his pace, I mine,
though once I could work through
a row with any man.

I admire Tom the
closeness of his motion,
sparing shoulders and back.
He brings the same to carpentry,
can drive a twenty-penny nail
straight through seasoned oak.
On rainy, damp days
he builds little twig fires
to warm himself while
doing chores, and once he
burned his own house down.

Already I feel the strain
in my back and the work's
not halfway done.
I'll work on awhile
chopping out the chokeweed
and wild grass to give
the knee-high plants space
to spread their own green lives.

Tom and I bow gently
over our hoes
to the field, to each other,
and to the work
that can still be done.

Alpheus Waters

JULY 12, 1882

I am eight again,
in my first boots
tramping about, setting
snares and baiting traps,
more animal than boy,
more like someone struggling
than one who is beginning
to live the life he loves.
At night I pick cotton
around a log fire or
sit by the barn roasting
potatoes while my
father fires tobacco.
By day I haul water
with cart and oxen
from Warren's spring,
or go on horseback
with a bag of corn
down to Stephen's mill
on Whippoorwill Creek,
or listen to Uncle Josh Horn
whose preaching at Oak Grove
strangely moves me so that
a life from the dead
rushes through me
and changes me.
After the sermon I
go up to my cousins
Robert and Tim

who will die at Shiloh
but they are afraid
and run away.

Who is this boy
has fathered
forth the man
I have become?
The sixty years
between us bends
and shifts and doubles
back like a river
running quietly before me.
I wait to discover in him
what I once was
and what I still may be.

Alpheus Waters

JULY 13, 1882

Suckering is almost
beyond me now.
Working each plant from
top to bottom for the
small gummy shoots
one for every leaf
in the hot August sun
is some of the hardest
work I've ever done.
My chest fills with the
stooping heat, the air
beneath the leaves moves
only with my motion.
I cannot see Tom or his
son Abe where they work.
Each of us moves in a
little space bounded narrowly
by tall plants and broad leaves.
Even the shade is hot.

Heat thickens around me,
minutes come faster
bumping into one another
in their hurry to be done.
The tobacco stands over me
breathing as I breathe,
its exhaling full of sweet narcotic.
My lungs and skin burn with it.
The air shimmering with heat and

light
lifts me out of myself.
I try to stand and call to Tom
but the dirt between the rows
quickens with the revolving earth.
My chest explodes.

Anne Waters

I am being pulled
along the surface
of still water by
something heavy moving
down deep where
light ends and
cool darkness rises
from a rocky floor.
The hook is set deep
within me, close against
the bone. The hard line
goes taut and water
snaps away in beads.
When my shadow moves
I must go too,
though it dives further
than the line can play
and faster than my
breath can follow.
Then the shore of this world
which seems so solid
and so new
will be a watery
dream that I will
soon forget, becoming
a part of currents
while clouds of fish
will drift between
the sun and me.

Anne Waters
SEPTEMBER 1, 1882

I walk out to watch
the same sky fill
itself with light
that he and I
had studied
ten thousand times
to guess the
weather's intentions.
We were tied
to land and sky
all our lives
and now I'm left
between them
to watch alone
each day
the same sun
climbing its bright stairs.
Everything around me
speaks of loss,
the hollow of our bed,
our fields of corn
and wheat,
the meadow grass
beneath my feet.
Even tobacco
hanging in the barn
repeats the message
of the slowly disappearing creek.

Anne Waters

SEPTEMBER 7, 1882

This fall comes early
and hard.
Ears of uncut corn
drop in the dry fields
and tobacco withers
silently in the barn.
Already
in the heart
of the hackberry tree
five chosen leaves
turn red as blood
and the light takes
on a fearful intensity.
In the evening
I walk through the
fields down to where
the river goes
into the ground.
Once I heard her voice
in the falling water.
I don't believe it
will be silent now.
He is wherever I look,
in the horse lot,
in the barn,
and on my eyes
like a light-fed image
that will not fade.
What does nature know

of those who've entered her,
or of us who still work
and walk about the world?
Perhaps those who die
do not drop out of the world.
They remain.
The world takes them,
and they are changed.